CW00421095

by David Taylor

Foreword by
Michael Matthews

A short poem by a most grateful benificiary of the L.A.T.C.H. organisation,
12 year old Lee Evans of Port Talbot

'Fighting Cancer'

Cancer, that word we fear to say,
I am fighting day by day.
I miss my mates, they are all in school
I miss my lessons, as a rule.
I have new hospital friends you see
But they are all the same as me.
The days are long when you're stuck indoors
Especially when you are feeling sore.
I will beat CANCER, I hope and cry
I'll battle through, I'll always try.

Old Bakehouse Publications

Abertillery

ISBN 1 874538 57 3

Published in the U.K. by
Old Bakehouse Publications
Church Street,
Abertillery, Gwent NP13 lEA
Telephone: 01495 212600 Fax: 01495 216222

Made and printed in the UK
by J.R. Davies (Printers) Ltd.

Foreword
by
Michael Matthews

First things first, the proceeds of this book will go to support an excellent charity L.A.T.C.H. as a tribute to the wonderful work Llandough Hospital does and will continue to do. This book has been compiled by an old pupil of mine David Taylor, who seeks to repay in some measure for the work the hospital has done for him personally, an excellent endeavour.

The book is a celebration in photographs, of memories on Pantside and the surrounding areas of the old Abercarn Urban District. Chapter 5 also has wonderful memories of the pupils, teachers and non-teaching staff of Greenfield Secondary Modern School, Newbridge, a great school where I started my teaching career in 1967, and continued until my retirement in 1997, after the school had amalgamated with Newbridge Grammar School and continued as Newbridge Comprehensive School.

The years at Greenfield hold many wonderful memories for me, I have been lucky to have made lifelong friends among both pupils and staff.

The people of Newbridge are both warm-hearted and generous. I think I can speak for all past staff of Greenfield School to have felt privileged to have spent time among them.

My memories of Greenfield are numerous - far too numerous to even begin to illuminate, but I would like to claim a small part in the meeting of David, the author, and Susan his wife. It was at a school outward bound week at Hilston Park that Susan and David first got together.

As I write these few lines many faces flash before my eyes, some here, some sadly not, but all bound together by the time we spent at a school where I believe we all cared for one another, both staff and pupils.

Greenfield was, I believe that excellent thing, a place where people cared, if there were problems they would soon be forgiven and forgotten.

It gives me great personal pride to hear, "hello sir", in the supermarket, in the street, in the garden centre, or in the pub, even when the voice is sometimes of someone not too many years older than myself.

Mike Matthews

Contents

Introduction

This book deals with some of the towns and villages once under the authority of the now disbanded Abercarn Urban District Council. The region, set within the valley of the River Ebbw accommodates amongst others, such places as Crumlin, Newbridge and Abercarn itself, these being quite important towns in the former industrial times of the nineteenth century.

Overlooking this assiduous area was the spacious green and pastoral land belonging to the Llanover Estate. During the period following World War Two however, with industry thriving with recovery, a natural and steady increase in population prevailed, causing an inevitable shortage of new housing. Thus it was, that eyes were cast upon the 'green and pleasant land' of Mynydd Maen with a view to creating a modern and extensive housing estate. A generous portion was eventually purchased by the Urban Council and so the area to be known as Pantside began developing in the early 1950s.

The book provides a photographic account of as much of the district as possible, of its people and past industrial wealth. Obviously, Pantside being the 'newest addition' to the family of towns, is lacking in great quantity of historical pictures although those scenes included do confirm a once-rural setting. Community spirit in Pantside however, has seen exceptional development during its forty-year lifespan and I have included a wide selection to prove the point. All the necessary ingredients such as education, religious worship and social interests have been presented.

The 'not too far away' hamlet of Hafodyrynys receives worthy attention and further down the valley, the towns of Crumlin and Newbridge are examined with telling pictures. Pictures of the once-mighty viaduct, crossing the valley some two hundred feet above the ground, offer a reminder to more mature readers of the active railway links that served the valley until 1964. The most vital component in the area's economy was of course the mining of coal; the collieries of Celynen, Newbridge providing work for thousands for more than a hundred years. To feed from this economy it was necessary for numbers of shops and services to be available in the High Street, many of which have since disappeared, as noted in some of the photographs. Numerous sporting champions have emanated from the district and they too have been given adequate mention.

The final chapter deals with Abercarn and Cwmcarn. The area was at one time a hive of industrial workings that included the 18th-century blast furnace; the important tin works and the ill-fated Prince of Wales Colliery, which claimed hundreds of lives during its lifetime. Abercarn has been quite transformed since the phasing out of older industries, to be replaced with modern production units. Many of the town's places of worship, entertainment and ancient dwellings such as 'The Ranks' have now been razed to the ground and a modern roadway disguises the previous landscape. Fortunately a number of old pictures have survived and they serve to illustrate those interesting and important times.

I have tried to include a wide range of topics in this latest book, hopefully providing many hours of reflection for its readers.

Finally, I am personally indebted to the services provided by Llandough Hospital, Cardiff, and as part of my gratitude, my own proceeds from the sale of this book are to be donated to the L.A.T.C.H. appeal.

David Taylor.

CHAPTER 1
The Origins of Pantside

The general area of Pantside was, up until 1952, a pleasant, gently sloping, part agricultural and part wooded south westerly extension of Mynydd Maen; a mountain ridgeway that separated the eastern and western valleys of the old county of Monmouthshire. The Welsh 'Pant' is translated as a valley or hollow and this wooded hollow can be seen in the photograph below, in the top right-hand corner. This was the scene prior to the building of the estate, Pant being situated to the east of Newbridge. Newbridge is a small but well-established town in the Ebbw Valley that grew with the coal industry that once monopolised the economy of the district; it being some ten miles from the once important shipping services of Newport. Politically, Newbridge was under the auspices of Abercarn Urban District Council. After the end of the Second World War in 1945, the country faced a chronic housing shortage and the Ebbw Valley was not to be omitted from that situation. Consequently the Abercarn U.D.C. surveyed their areas and eventually decided that the slopes rising from the bottom of the Pant would make an ideal site for housing construction.

1. A view of Pantside before the building of the housing estate.

The land at the time was in the ownership of the Llanover Estate and in August 1952 the council completed the purchase for the sum of £3365. At the lower end of the Pant ran the Crumlin arm of the Monmouthshire Canal, it having been unused and neglected for many years. The canal now much overgrown and weed-infested, was a natural habitat for flora and fauna, now long gone.

This western branch of the canal was built by Thomas Dadford and opened in 1799. The route followed the Ebbw Valley from Crumlin, on to Rogerstone then eastwards to meet the Eastern Valley branch at Crindau near Newport. Thomas Dadford Jnr. is buried at Llanarth near Abergavenny, his gravestone being inscribed '*In Memory of Thomas Dadford late of Crickhowell in the County of Brecknok, Engineer who departed this life April 2nd 1801 Aged 40 Years*'.

One of the access routes to the new building site was over the green bridge where once stood an old canal lock and lock-keeper's cottage.This was a very narrow route leading into Pant Road where clearances were very tight, presenting problems for vehicles in not damaging old buildings on either side. Another access to the site was via a narrow hump-backed bridge over the canal and about a hundred metres from this bridge is the ancient Pant Farm. To the left of this farm was a dirt-track road, known today as Old Pant Road; this being one of a number of such routes connecting other local farms and isolated small-holdings.

2. Taken from the same spot as the previous photograph, this is how the scene appears in the 1990s.

Immediately behind Pant Farm and on a higher level is the imposing White House, 'Llwyncelyn' meaning 'Holy Grove or Bush' which is understood to have been the residence of the colliery owner's agent Ben Owen. Opposite to the entrance to the White House is a pathway leading to a wooded area known locally as Hospital Wood, Coed Goferau (wood of the streams).This is where the isolation hospital was built before the First World War, where victims of contagious diseases could receive treatment.

The hospital was situated to the left of the large white house, as seen in the near centre of the above photograph. Also quite close by was an old cottage, the ruins of which are still to be seen today. Further up the hill the ground levelled off onto a plateau and to the right is an area known as Tir-y-Pwll (Land of the Pond or Pool). Standing here is a large house named 'Ty-Pwll' which was built in 1921 and presently owned by Mr. and Mrs. Hodges. To the side of this property are Tir-y-Pwll Cottages and small-holding which are thought to date back some 400 years. The bottom cottage was originally a barn before being converted in about 1922 by Mr. Matt Williams; the original cottage was owned by members of the Bolton family for many years.

The bottom dwelling and small-holding was owned and farmed in 1945 by Mr. Jack Haines, a well-respected local shepherd on Mynydd Maen Common. This area is known locally as 'The Moors or Whinberry Mountain'. The property is now owned by Mr. Haines' son Roger who carries on the family tradition of sheep farming on Mynydd Maen and Twyn-y-Gnoll.

The Twyn-y-Gnoll (an 1846 Tithe Map offering the spelling Ganoll) area, lies beneath the very large South Celynen spoil tip overlooking Pantside. Below this tip was Upper Gnoll Farm at Pen-Rhiw-Fawr and some small cottage holdings, Gnoll Fach, Twyn-y-Ganoll. Gnoll Farm was in the capable hands of the Smith family from 1926 until early 1938. Alongside this farmstead ran a very old parish cart-road, known as the Green Path. The footpath travels up from the Graig at the bottom of the Pant, onto the mountain top over the plateau of Mynydd Maen to the eastern side of the valley. Immediately behind this large spoil tip lies another small upland farm, Hafod Fach (Little Summer House or Small Summer Dwelling). There are historical records indicating that Hafod Fach, like a number of other local farms, was used for services of Baptism during the early 1800s, in the absence of a proper place of Baptist worship. (There is local legend that the dwelling is haunted by the strange sound of an old church organ playing during unearthly hours of the night!).

7

3. A familiar scene at Ysgubor-Wen on Mynydd Maen in 1964 with John Herbert and Jack Haines gathering the sheep.

Near to where Ellesmere Court is situated today, stood an old wooden bungalow which was occupied for some time by a Mrs. Richards. Immediately behind this bungalow is Lower Cefn Rhos-y-Bedd Farm, owned by the Llanover Estate and farmed by the Herbert family for many years; Mr. Herbert was also a well-known local auctioneer. The farm was later transferred to Mr. and Mrs. Eric Sayes, with Mrs. Sayes still occupying the property. Cefn-Rhos-y-Bedd may be translated as 'Ridge of the Moorland Grave' or perhaps 'Back of the Grave on the Moor'.

4. A typical rural photograph from the early 1930s showing sheep shearers gathered at the Gnoll Farm, Pen-Rhiw-Fawr, and included in the picture are - Back: Mr. Collins, Jack Haines, Bob Smith, Dai Hopkins, Jim Turner, Matt Reynolds, unknown and Fan the dog. Front: Bill Smith, unknown and the young lad is Jim Hawkesford.

Further up the hill and another farm is reached, this is Cefn-Rhos-y-Bedd Ucaf (Upper), once owned by Mr. and Mrs. Lewis. Just past the entrance to this farm is the crossroads with the lane to the right leading to the mountain top; the path to the left leads down The Rhiw to where once stood Mill Brook Cottages at Crumlin. This ancient pathway was at one time the route of an old cart road and straight ahead will be found the lane to Hafodyrynys village. On the lane, about half way up towards the mountain top, on the left-hand side, is a public right of way; this was at one time used as a pony and cart road that connected with various other such lanes and pathways. The area where the pathway still travels down through into Hafodyrynys was once known as Tir Watkin (Watkins' Land). Many years ago, in the early part of the nineteenth century, there was another old house and croft occupied by a brother and sister, Daniel and Leah Philips. Immediately on the right-hand side another farm entrance is to be seen, this leading to Blaengwrney Farm (Source of the Stream). This mountain stream (Nant Gawni) flows down through a beautiful, natural and unspoilt wooded dingle to the bottom of Pant and into the River Ebbw. The farm at Blaengwrney was built around 1884 although there were much earlier farm buildings here. Originally Mr. and Mrs. Vicary came to work the farm in February 1946 and both father and son were presented with The Prince Of Wales Award for their skilled craftsmanship in dry-stone walling on Mynydd Maen Common. The last farm on the left-hand side, before the mountain top is reached is Pen-y-Caeau (Top Of The Fields) and now owned by Byron and Gail Williams.

5. Mrs. Hawkesford (nee Smith) is to be seen at Gnoll Farm in the early 1930s. Mr. and Mrs. Hawkesford also lived at the Trwyn Farm and the Gnoll Cottage. By 1938 it was necessary to move down to Ty-Pwll, due to the amount of unwelcomed dust that was now polluting the area from the tip belonging to the South Celynen Colliery.

6. John Powell (Powell the Lock) at work on the canal at the bottom of the Pant about 1910. The last narrow boat that travelled from Crumlin to Newport was in 1930.

7. Seen here is the Green Bridge which crossed over the canal at the bottom of Pant. The Crumlin arm of the canal finally closed in 1949.

8. This small farm house (Pant Farm) at the bottom of Pant Side, has a history stating that the dwelling is between two and three hundred years old, possibly older.

9. A photograph of Pantside that was taken in March 1950. Some features to be noted are Ty-Pwll House and cottages with the wooden bungalow, occupied by Mrs. Richards in the middle distance.

10. One of the final little hillside landmarks to be found during a mountain walk is the cattle grid, this providing access to the mountain top of Mynydd Maen Urban Common (Mountain of Stones); the local name given is Whinberry Mountain. On this photograph can be seen Cil-Lonydd Farm (Silent Quiet Retreat). This moorland- looking area is where the twelfth-century monks of Llantarnam Abbey travelled on their pilgrimages to Penrhys, which runs past Llanderfel Gelli-Gravog and up the shoulder of Mynydd Maen. Cil-Llonydd was a grange farm belonging to Llantarnam Abbey which was founded in about 1171. The property consisted of a number of ancillary buildings to house the lay brothers who worked the farm. A chapel also stood close by, the area bearing the ancient name of Cae-Eglwys or Cae Chapel.

Some centuries later, with the disappearance of the religious order, the farm was converted into a commercial undertaking. In the early 1970s Mr. Dennis Lewis began developing the site as a tourist attraction, a pony trekking centre; this later expanding with the addition of a licensed premises to be known as The Double D Pub. The venture proved popular and successful until 1984 when the all-out miners' strike affected the economy of the area so badly. In the aftermath of this, the Centre did not recover and the amenities finally closed on December 31st 1986.

In the late 1930s a nine-hole golf course was also built on the fields of Cil-Lonydd with an accompanying clubhouse. The advent of war in 1939 prevented further development here and today all evidence of the course has vanished.

11./12. Two views of Trwyn Farm with Mrs. Emily Hawkesford seen on the lower photograph quietly relaxing on the dry-stone wall. The farm in the past earned itself a reputation for strange happenings, attributable to infrequent visits by a ghostly figure answering to the name of 'Pwkar Trwyn'. The name Pwkar still attracts some conversation in certain parts of the County of Gwent.

13. The Trwyn which, until the 1920s, served as a working farm. The property was then acquired by the Forestry Commission and converted into tied cottages. The lady on the right of this photograph is Sadie Jones who lived with her father Ben at the farm.

14. Cil-Lonydd farm which is seen in a state of ruin in 1997. The farm has a history dating back to the 13th Century when it belonged to Llantarnam Abbey before being seized by Henry VIII with all its lands. In 1949, the then occupier Mr. Arthur Blake, ploughed up some ancient swords which now reside in the National Museum of Wales. Following Mr. Blake's residency, locals may also remember Dennis Lewis and family who farmed the property for some thirty years.

15. An aerial view of Pantside Housing Estate that provides interesting study with a number of features to look for. In the centre is the roundabout surrounded by St. Peter's Church, the shops, the school and to the right Tir-y-pwll flats.

16. A general view of Pant Housing Estate as it looked during the late 1950s. It will be noticed that the area in the top right hand corner has yet to be developed, the new houses not arriving until the early 1970s. On the extreme bottom left was the pre-fabricated shop and local residents will remember Mr. Grove Burris occupying one side and Mr. Glyn Thomas other. This site now houses St. Peter's Close and a home for the elderly.

17. This is another view from the 1960s that has seen a few changes since. The main road leading up the hill is Central Avenue and just visible behind the three houses on the right, is old Pant Farm once owned by Mr. and Mrs. Teddy Edwards. In the far distance is Pen-Rhiw-Bicca which is part of Newbridge, all this area is seen before construction of the new southern by-pass from Newbridge to Maesycwmmer.

CHAPTER 2

Worship & Schooling at Pantside

18. St. Peter's Church Pantside (the daughter church of St. Paul's Newbridge) which was officially opened for worship in March 1960.

Pantside being a relatively new housing estate and community, was not blessed with places of historical worship as were the more established surrounding villages. Consequently, by popular demand and desire in the mid 1950s, Reverend Stanley Jones the incumbent of St. Paul's Church Newbridge came to the rescue. It was his inspiration that led to the ideas of providing a church for the residents of the Pant Estate.

The first building was little more than a wooden hut which fronted onto Central Avenue where the gates to the present church now stand. The good people of Pant were to give generously over the next few years, with many a door to door collection and fund-raising activity. Eventually targets were reached and sufficient monies were accumulated to allow the building of the much improved church that stands today. The completed place of worship was officially opened by the Archbishop of Wales, The Most Reverend Alfred Edwin Morris on Wednesday March 9th 1960. Like many religious institutions in these closing years of the twentieth century, their numbers of followers have declined and St. Peter's at Pantside has seen its 'ups and downs'. The once so-popular annual Whitsun March around the district by the Sunday School children is also a victim of the declining interest; the church however is still a central point for social gatherings, in addition to the normal religious services endeavouring to maintain a place in the local community.

19. The occasion is the laying of the Foundation Stone at St. Peter's on July 23rd 1959 by Mr. L.T. Edwards. Also in the picture are The Archbishop of Wales and Reverend Stanley Jones of Newbridge.

18

20. A group of 'Young Wives' belonging to St. Peter's pictured during the early 1960s and here are a few familiar names to remember - May Cooke, Pat Callaghan, Mrs. Burge, Elizabeth Davies, Mrs. Harvey, Mrs. Stone, Miss Davies, Barbara Sheppard, Poppy Paynter, Glenys and Ann Webster, Bessie Boulton, Peg Greedy, Emily Hawkesford, Mrs. Davies, Mrs. Long and Mrs. Williams.

21. A Whitsun March at Pantside with the church in the background shortly after the opening in 1960.

22. Another view of a 1960s Whitsun March with the banner held high. Hopefully there are some local residents who will be able to recognise a few faces seen here.

23. The opening day at St. Peter's is further celebrated by the choir at Pantside School, the choristers being led on this occasion by Robert Richards.

24. The official opening of a new church would not be complete without a celebratory tea and here are the ladies who helped provide the necessary refreshments on the day at Pantside School. Back row, left to right: Mrs. Jennifer Dugmore (nee Purnell), Mrs. Val Hodges (nee Hawkesford). Front row: Mrs. Harvey, Mrs. Bessie Boulton, Mrs. Bird, Mrs. Emily Hawkesford, Mrs. Elizabeth Davies, Mrs. Stone, Mrs. Porter, Mrs. Strange and Mrs. Hatherall.

25. Suitably attired for a traditional Christmas concert at the school are these local children from about 1959. Front Row: Eileen Winkle, Carol Wozencroft, Robert Davies, John Welch, Gareth Richards, Kenneth Francis, Raymond Lias, John Pearn, Karen Hillman, Wendy West. Second Row: Ann Mainwaring, Christine Price, Philip Watkins, Stephen Jackson, Terry Young, Peter Saunders, Barrie Dorman, Bernard Knott, John Kellow, Kenneth Whitcombe. Third Row: Lyn Wilkins, Anne Edmunds, Lynette Shipp, Sandra Jeremiah, Hazel Jones and Malcolm Scott as Mary and Joseph, Lynda Williams, Christine Johns, Elizabeth Yemm. Back Row: Patricia Coles, Barbara Lewis, Lesley Shepherd, Kathleen Hicks, Lynette Daley, Karen Roache, Kathleen Barbero, Gwyneth Jones, Dawn Bevan.

26. Pantside Estate with the Primary School in the middle distance. This school was first planned as a one-form entry Junior and Infants' with capacity for 280 children in early 1956. The scheme was finally approved by the Ministry of Education in October of that year with building commencing in the summer of 1957 by Messers Arthur and Sons of Maesycwmmer. The first pupils were accepted at the start of the Autumn Term September 1st 1958. A total of 118 children from the Pantside area who had previously been obliged to attend the junior schools at Pentwynmawr, Tynewydd, Newbridge (Greenfield) and Crumlin were now enrolled. The teaching staff at the time consisted of Mr. Thomas Brown Hayward as headmaster, assisted by Mr. Attwood, Miss Lloyd together with the occasional services of Mrs. Evans and Mrs. Williams. It is likely that there are some readers of this book who attended the school during this period and would of course, now be in their 'Forties' but will still remember their first day at Junior School and the names and faces of their earliest teachers. The official opening was held over until October 7th 1958, the well-attended ceremony being performed by County Councillor W.J. King.

27. The year is 1964 and teacher Miss Beddoes joins headmaster Mr. Lewis for a class photograph. Reading left to right the pupils are - Front: Julie Sergeant, Kathleen Davies, Rose West, Linda Brown, Lesley Morgan, Susan Mathews and Yvonne Hughes. Middle: Billy Harris (Artex), Leonard Wallace, Linda Coombes, Pat Jones, Margaret Daley, Richard Wilkins and Steve Madden. Back: Alan Thomas, Steve Belt and Andrew Long.

28. There are fifty-two pupils here in about 1964 and it has not been possible to name them all with certainty. However here are a few to look out for, starting from the back. Janet Bray, Janet McGow, Jennifer Dee, Norma Protheroe, Meryl Rees, Janet Wigg, Ann Webster, Janice Williams, Angela Leonard, Lesley Sheppard, Diane Phillips, Janet Otter, Susan Davies, Marina Smith, Janice Hopkins, Marion Poole, Elaine Groves, Angela De Marco, Kim Jones, Susan Noakes, Michael Lane, Derek Hart, Steven Hart, Robert Carnell, Peter Speed, Phil Leader, John James, Robert Adams, Steven Saunders, Steven Jones, Clive Carter, Linda Coombes, Linda Brown, Pat Jones, Judith Rossiter, Janice Walker, Alison Fiddy, Elizabeth Thompson, Susan Thomas, June Harris, Lynette Jenkins, Kathleen Davies, Sharon Williams, Cynthia Beach, Susan Thomas and Julie Sergeant.

29. This time it's the turn of some members of staff to be pictured at the school and included are Mr. Crowley, Mr. Thomas, Mrs. Sutton, Mr. Lewis (Headmaster), Muriel Lloyd, Miss Beddows, Marjorie Morgan and Dorothy Lock.

30. From the mid 1960s comes another school photograph with teacher Mr. Thomas and Head, Mr. Lewis present. Among the many pupils to be identified by readers are Gareth Owens, Russell Stevens, Steven Henry, Paul Parry, Carole Thomas, Angela James, Judith Gundy, Susan Degendorfer, Angela Jackson, Gaynor Lewis, Angela Richards, Theresa Noakes, Christine English, Cheryl Hodge, Susan Leadbeater, Andrew Shepherd, Steven Davies and Gareth Griffiths.

31. The year is thought to be 1965 and seen left to right are - Front: Gaynor Frost, Rosemary Long, Eirwen Gibbons, Janice Edmunds, Joy Thomas, Gloria Wilkins and Denise Booton. Middle: Ian Morgan, Wayne Parry, Marcia Lucas, Susan Richards, Carole Galloway, Denise Pearce, Helena Davies, Michael Belt and Perry Saunders. Back: Robert English, Kevin Lane, Neil Jones, Alan Hughes and Steven Davey.

32. The year is now 1964 and time for another Christmas concert at the infants' school. Unfortunately it has not been possible to account for all the names but here are a few to look for - Dean Walker, Beverley Morris, Jill Ball, Peter Smith, Kevin Andrews, Michael Hawker, Glenys Saunders, Perry Saunders, Kevin Lane, Graham Heath, Helena Davies, Gaynor Frost, Anthony Weekes, Robert Whatley and Wayne Bowden.

33. Pantside Junior School in 1968 with Mr. Lewis stood on the left and fellow teacher Miss Thomas on the right. The youngsters can be recognised as follows - Front: Pat Rees, Barbara Hughes, Patricia Hart, Cheryl Ellis, Anita Beacham, Diane Parker, Jane Partridge and Joanne Jones. Middle: Gary Thomas, Gerald Evans, Christopher Hopkins, Terry Maggs, Diane Daniels, John Freeman, and Huw Roberts. Back: Mark Holbrook, Heather James, Pamela Wilkins, Gaynor Brown, Robert Whatley, Leighton Breeze and Jill Madden.

34. A photographic record of Pantside Junior School from about 1969. Mr. Jones the headmaster is on the left; with a student and form teacher Mr. Beyton. The youngsters seen left to right are as follows - Back: Paul Beccham, Graham Heath, Wayne Parry, Perry Saunders, David Taylor, Wayne Coles, Susan Richards, Rosemary Long and Robert Griffiths. Third Row: Beverley Harris, Steven Jones, Michael Belt, Kevin Lane, Jonathan Wilkes, Peter Smith, Michael Davies, Gwyn Leonard and Jeanette James. Second Row: Jane Partridge, Cheryl Ellis, Deborah Thomas, Jane Webb, Diane Parker, Jane Baber, Susan Peck and Helena Davies. Front: Robert Whatley, Lynne Beech, David Williams, Peter Williams, Glyn Phillips and Keith Ballsdon.

35. The deserving 'Dinner Ladies' and staff pose for a photograph in the 1970s. At the back are Doreen James, Joyce Moxley (Headmistress) and Pamela Davies. Front: Mavis Davies, Pat James, Mr. Milton Jones (Headmaster), Olwyn Vaughan (Head Cook) and Marion Leonard. Inset shows an ex-dinner lady from Pantside School, Mrs. Edmunds who in 1999 celebrated her 100th birthday.

36. The Pantside Junior Football Team during the 1969-1970 season. With Mr. Jones on the left and Mr. Beyton on the right, the boys are - Back: Gary Thomas, Graham Heath, David Taylor, Alan Whitcombe, Wayne Coles, John Otter and Christopher Hopkins. Middle: Gwyn Leonard, Terry Phillips, Kevin Lane, Robert Haines and Wayne Parry. Front: Christopher Parker and Neil Jones.

37. Another collection of pupils with their tutors in the 1960s. Left to right the boys and girls include - Back: Helen Parry, Timothy Miles, Steven Hopkins, Carl Rogers, Wayne James and Heather James. Middle: Timothy McGow, Timothy Mills, Ian Watkins, Jonathan Wilks, Robert Griffiths, Alan Sayes, Steven Dale, Christopher Parker, John Otter and Steven Jones. Front: Anita Beacham, Patricia Hart, Janet Davies, Helen Capper, Deborah Davies, Lynette James, Jane Partridge, Susan Heath, Kerry Morris and Jill Ball. The staff members are Mrs. Venn and Mr. Milton Jones.

38. The juniors with headmaster Mr. Jones and teacher Mr. Crowley on the far right. The youngsters from the 1960s are - Back: Lorraine Castree, Rosemary Long, Kay Gougerty, Janice Edmonds, Tracey Eyles, Carole Lambert, Jane Jones, Meryl Carnell, Eirwen Gibbons, Beverley Hall, Susan Richards and Kerry Hyde. Middle: Wayne Coles, Mark Gomoluch, Alan Hughes, Gary White, Robert Barnes, ?, Alan Whitcombe, Kevin Lane, Stephen Davey, Robert English, Stephen Harrington and Ian Morgan. Front: Lynne Beech, David Williams, ?, Sandra Hart, Denise Pearce, Gloria Wilkins, Gaynor Frost, Denise Booten, Lynne Pope, Anthony Morris and Neil Jones.

39. The years have now moved on to 1984 and Mr. Chantry and Mr. Thomas accompany some pupils who include - Richard Davies, Lee Gibbons, Tony Langley, Shane Harlin, Lee Protheroe, Mark Tudor, Natalie Freeman, Craig Thomas, Alison East, Mark Hughes, Paul Taylor, Melanie Jones, Caroline Purnell, Claire Derrick, Sally Lowman, Joanne Shepherd, Derek Hammett and Kirk Greenslade.

40. Traditional Welsh costume is the order of the day on March 1st, St. David's Day each year in the Welsh valleys. Here are some examples from 1993 at Pantside Primary. Left to right are Julie Dainton, Nicky Taylor, Leila Dee, Barry Taylor and Melissa Jones.

41. The year is again 1993 with headmaster Mr. Keith Jones on the left and Mr. Roger Morris on the right. The children are - Back: Gareth Lovell, Liam Jennings, Barry Taylor, Joshua Watkins, Daniel Morgan, James Molyneux, Gavin Edwards and Dean James. Third Row: Emma Walkley, Natalie Shepherd, Leila Dee, Leanne Vicary, Tony Strickland, Natasha Cook and Linsey Bodily. Second Row: Kate Greenslade, Danielle Booten, Katherine Degendorfer, Kelly Palmer, Julie Dainton, Amy Carver, Rachael Barnes and Melissa Jones. Front: Damien Tyler, Nathan Rees and Craig Davies.

42. It is 1994 at the school and time for the staff to be photographed. In the back row are Mrs. Jennifer Morris, Mrs. Jennifer Rowlands, Mrs. Susan Parham, Mrs. Carolyn Edmunds, Mrs. Carol Erasmus, Mrs. Claire Thomas and Miss Penny Barter. Front: Mr. Roger Morris, Mrs. Christine Vaughan, Mr. Keith Jones (Head Teacher), Mrs. Rosemary Stephens and Mrs. Kerylyn Steer (School Secretary).

43. The final school photograph is of the infants in 1993 flanked by Mrs. Jennifer Morris and Mr. Keith Jones. Back: Carla Price, Charlotte Ford, Sophie Williams, Roxanne Gilbert, Nadine Tyler, Katie Llewellyn and Kylie Jo Smith. Third Row: Aaron Clements, Ryan Lane, Jason Waite, Tyrone Freyne, Christopher Miles, Nicky Taylor, Jonathan Stredwick and Darren Parker. Second Row: Jenny Collins, Carrie Ann Severn, Laura Cook, Rebecca Grubb, Cheryl Price, Alicia Selway and Christine Vicary. Front: Kyle Gilbert and Jamie Harrington.

CHAPTER 3

Sport, Entertainment & Pantside People

44. A Pantside R.F.C. team on the field during the 1980-81 season. In the back row are Jim Pooke, Don Woodward, Haydn Rees, David Allford, Richard Wanklyn, Norman Florence, Dennis Parfitt, Caleb West, Gary Francis, Graham Shipp, Alan Rees and Brian Hughes. Front: Bob Shepherd, Grayson Haines, Philip Churcher, Mark Guider, Philip Hipkiss, Bill Clark, Alwyn Jones and Graham Hughes.

45. The late Malcolm Rogers of Old Pant Road, Pantside, is seen at the wheel of his Mark One Ford Cortina at the Crefft Rally in 1977. A great enthusiast of motor rallying, locals may also remember him as a former owner of the Flyover Garage in Aberbeeg.

46. Pantside A.F.C. during the successful season of 1971-72 when they were League and Cup Winners as evidenced by the trophies on display. The team members are - Back: S. Daniels, P. Leader, A. Long, P. Speed, C. Brass and J. Harris. Middle: A. Brass, G. Smith, A. Case and G. Roberts. Front: R. Carnell and I. Smith.

47. Pantside A.F.C. pictured when they were winners of the Tom Perkins Cup in 1996-97 and seen left to right the players are - Back: Ian Bray, Steve Hughes, Lee Richards, Paul Morgan, Mark Hughes, Mike Thorne and Andrew Gregory. Front: Kieron Protheroe, Phil Purnell, Chris Long, Stuart Aston (captain), Mark Protheroe, Wayne Yearsley and Neil Lewis. The dependable subs are Anthony Protheroe, Chris Brown, Neil Jones and Glen Collins. Also pictured are Ernie Lewis (manager) and Bob Evans (physio).

48. An 'Under 12s' local football team from 1977 with committee members and trainers. Back Row: Tony Yearsley, Bob Davies, George Perry and Ossie Dorman. Middle: Steve Selway, Martin Powell, Robert Jones, Paul Davies, Mark Thomas and Eddie Molyneux. Front: Steve Wells, Paul Dienko, Kevin Dorman, Wayne Yearsley and Steve Perry.

49. The Pantside A.F.C. team during the 1974-75 season. Back Row: Alf Shepherd, Ian Jones, Geoff Miller, Andrew Long, John Bigham, Jimmy Winkle, Peter Speed, Colin Brass, Jeff Harris and George Rees. Front: Phil Williams, Michael Lane, John Kinsey, Alan Thomas and Phil Leader. The mascot is a young Steve Cook.

50. An alternative sport for the skilled is clay pigeon shooting and here are members of the local club at Cil-Lonydd Farm in 1978. Gazing through the window are Marshall and Mavis King and amongst those outside the pub are - Dennis Lewis, John Daniels, Richard Lucas, Alan Brimfield, John Everson, Paul Daley, Bob Shepherd, Martin Jones, Cliff Barnes, Steve Lucas, Steven Belt, Chris Watkins, Philip Brimfield and John Dodds.

51. The year 1984 saw the prolonged miners' strike and rallying calls for economic help for the families affected. Here is a scene from a comic football match organised by Pantside Workingmen's Club to help raise funds, and the ladies are - Back: Margaret Churcher, Mary Booton, Denise Clark, Sue Presley, Sue Lambert, Ann Hillier, ·Sue Stinton, Julie Ball, Cynthia Cheshire, Wendy Hipkiss and Lynette Daley. Front: Lynn Gingell, Lorraine Hughes, Christine Hughes, Silika Hillier, Barbara Chard, Carol West, Jackie Hipkiss and Sally Blanche.

52. As with all good clubs and organisations the ladies' section plays an all important part and here is a 1960s group at Pantside Club. Standing from left to right are - Mary Booton, Mrs. Edwards, Brenda Filer, Molly Morgan, ?, Peggy Morgan, Glad Forward, Mrs. Blanche, ?, Marion Rogers, Margaret Cook, Margaret Williams, ?, Roslyn Gregory, Margaret Thomas and Mrs. Carter. Seated - Marion Gibbs, Mrs. Marion George, Mrs. Evelyn Coombes, Marion Case, Mrs. Thomas and Mrs. Evans. Front row, sat on floor are Evelyn Golding and Mrs. Ashman.

53. The entertainers here are all members of Pantside Investitutes Jazz Band as they appeared at the Newbridge Carnival and Fête in July 1972. The gentleman at the back is Andrew Padmore who is surrounded by Linda Maggs, Mandy Richards, Lorraine King, Meryl Carnell, Kathleen Elsdon, Beverley Davies, Pat Saunders, Lynette Slocombe, Carol Rees, Joy Lewis, Ellen Bennett, ?, Susan Richards, Kerry Slocombe, Kay Gougerty, Rosemary Long, Gaynor Frost, Margaret Powell, Angela Jackson and Carol Whatley.

54. This group of youngsters seen in Newlyn Road were winners of a Britannia carnival competition in the late 1960s and include the following - Back row: Mrs. Welch, Beryl King, Wendy Davies and Jillian Shipp. Middle row: Linda Maggs, Pat Saunders and Lorraine Daley. Front row: Denise Booton, Lorraine King, Susan Richards, Carol Lambert and Rosemary Long.

55. Another scene at Newlyn Road with a street party in progress and some of the ladies are Peggy Morgan, Angela Richards, Edith Richards, Pearl Rogers and Maureen Shipp.

56. The Queen's Silver Jubilee was celebrated nationally in 1977 and a competition to find a local Jubilee Queen was held at Pantside Social Club in June of that year. All young teenagers at the time, the contestants are - Back: Susan Heath, Gillian Brown, Carol Greenslade, Rose Davies, Angela Hyde, Jacqueline Hipkiss, Mandy Bowden and Debra Frost. Front: Michelle Harris, Wendy Pearce, Carol Whatley, Andrea Griffiths, Faye Bowden, Katrina Davies. Jean Pearn and Wendy Hipkiss.

57. The 50th Anniversary of VE Day saw jollification throughout the country in 1995 and this is a street party in Claremont Road organised by Margaret Churcher (Auntie Mag). Amongst the many are Julie and Rachel Gordon, Ivor Freeman, Betty and Cy Woodward, Sandra Wallace, Gavin Edwards, Louise Morgan, Pat Davies, Tony Strickland and Steven Hillman. During 1996-97 the 'Pre-Fabs' at Claremont Road were the first to be demolished to make way for new bungalows in the area.

58. The precise occasion is uncertain but it is a party being held in Claremont Road, possibly to mark the investiture of the Prince Of Wales in 1969. The partygoers include Diane Parker, Deborah Hopkins, Lynne Gibbons, Wendy Hipkiss, Lynne Watkins, Glenys Saunders, Robert Adams and Janet Bray.

59. Seen here are Mr. Walter Vicary and his son Howard engaged in the ancient craft of dry stone walling in 1980. Father and son were to receive the Prince Of Wales Award for their skilled work in building this wall at Mynydd Maen. Walter's other talent as a local poet is demonstrated in his work *'A Morning In Summer'*. Mr. Walter Vicary passed away over a year ago.

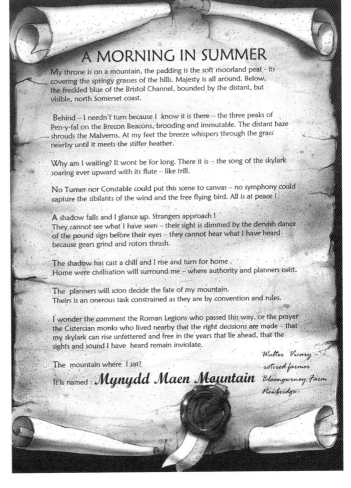

A MORNING IN SUMMER

My throne is on a mountain, the padding is the soft moorland peat - its covering the springy grasses of the hills. Majesty is all around. Below, the freckled blue of the Bristol Channel, bounded by the distant, but visible, north Somerset coast.

Behind – I needn't turn because I know it is there – the three peaks of Pen-y-fal on the Brecon Beacons, brooding and immutable. The distant haze shrouds the Malverns. At my feet the breeze whispers through the grass nearby until it meets the stiffer heather.

Why am I waiting? It wont be for long. There it is – the song of the skylark soaring ever upward with its flute – like trill.

No Turner nor Constable could put this scene to canvas – no symphony could capture the sibilants of the wind and the free flying bird. All is at peace !

A shadow falls and I glance up. Strangers approach ! They cannot see what I have seen – their sight is dimmed by the dervish dance of the pound sign before their eyes – they cannot hear what I have heard because gears grind and rotors thrash.

The shadow has cast a chill and I rise and turn for home . Home were civilisation will surround me – where authority and planners exist.

The planners will soon decide the fate of my mountain. Theirs is an onerous task constrained as they are by convention and rules.

I wonder the comment the Roman Legions who passed this way, or the prayer the Cistercian monks who lived nearby that the right decisions are made – that my skylark can rise unfettered and free in the years that lie ahead, that the sights and sound I have heard remain inviolate.

The mountain where I sat?

It is named : **Mynydd Maen Mountain**

Walter Vicary
retired farmer
Blaengwrney Farm
Newbridge

39

60. On the left is a young Kyle Davies of Newlyn Road Pant who brought some drama and excitement to St. Peter's Close in 1995. In search of a lost National Lottery ticket, the six-year-old became trapped in a waste bin causing some concern; the local Fire Brigade however came to the rescue and eventually freed him after a fifteen-minute exercise and a comforting cuddly toy as seen here.

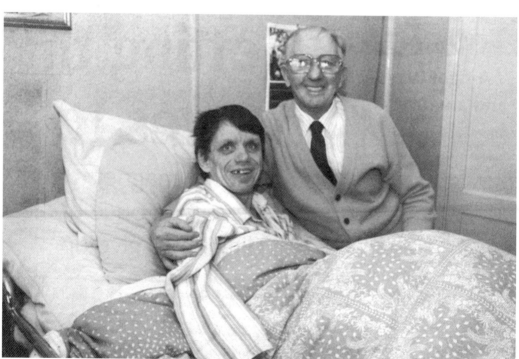

61. There are many familiar faces included in this book, perhaps none more so than Mr. John Shepherd and his disabled son Andrew. John's devotion to the non-stop care of his family earned him a most deserved 'Carer Of The Year Award' in 1995 which was presented by Islwyn Borough Council.

62./63. Once a 'watering hole' for many, was the Double D Public House at Cil-Lonydd and here are two photographs to remind readers. Amongst the crowd outside are Dennis and Doreen Lewis, Michael Davies, Gwyn Leonard, Eirwen Lewis, Bryn Wilkins, Gloria Wilkins, Walter Parfitt and Helen Lewis.

64. Another well-known face in the Pantside district and surrounding valleys was 'Danny The Ice Cream Man'. The relishing taste of Danny's home-made Italian styled ices will surely bring back a few memories to readers of this book.

65. The date is November 5th 1997 and a presentation is being made by Mrs. Doreen Roberts to Veronica Howells at the Pantside Post Office and shop; the occasion was to mark the Howells' family final day in this local business.

CHAPTER 4

In and around Newbridge

66. A view of High Street Newbridge that dates from the very earliest years of the twentieth century, around 1902. The corner building seen on the left was at one time the Tre Celyn Shop and nowadays the site of the HSBC Bank.

67. High Street looking in the opposite direction and some years later than the previous photograph. The period is very likely to be 1937 with a display of flags and bunting to celebrate the Coronation of King George VI in May of that year. On the right can be seen the once popular and busy store belonging to the Blaina Co-operative Society.

68. A scene from the 1950s of Victoria Terrace showing a number of businesses that have since left the town. The large shop on the left of the picture will be remembered as Gwyn Davies's for wallpaper and decorating materials, whilst on the right, was the Gas Showroom and in the distance Briggs for shoes and Mr. Salisbury the ironmongers shop.

69. Another view of old High Street Newbridge. Until the middle of the nineteenth century the area was described as a rural and pastoral land, that was of course prior to the discovery of rich coal deposits in the district. The name Newbridge or Cefn Bychan is said to have derived from a new and necessary bridge which was built over the River Ebbw in the 1790s.

70. The impressive store of Wallace Jones and Sons who traded in High Street Newbridge and a number of other valley towns. This picture was taken in 1955 during prosperous times before the arrival of 'out of town' superstores, an event that has all but annihilated old and established businesses such as Wallace Jones.

71. The Trecelyn Inn pictured during the 1960s when it was known as the Beaufort Arms Hotel. This inn was originally owned by the local family brewing company, Webbs of Aberbeeg who had been making fine beers for the valley pubs since 1838.

72. Tynewydd Terrace in days gone by with a number of once-busy shops. On the left is the corner of the Newbridge Hotel and opposite was Mrs. Marsh for fruit and veg, the Top Hat Club, Graham Cox the barber, Jack Flowers the butcher's, Bolwell's sweet shop and the Mayfair Pet shop.

73. Cwmdoes in about 1920 with a few long-forgotten features. The pavement outside the Red Lion is blocked with some old wooden beer barrels and further along, on the right, the old practice of having one's load of coal dumped at the front door is to be seen. Also pictured on the right is the old Supper Bar.

74. In the centre can be seen Tynewydd School which managed to achieve its centenary in 1996 shortly before demolition. At a higher level is Cae Twmpyn Park and also Newbridge cenotaph which was removed in recent times and re-located at St. Fagan's Cardiff. The top right of this photograph illustrates how the area appeared before Pantside was developed.

75. A panoramic view of an older-looking Newbridge which was taken from Morgan Edwards' Field. In the distance to the right of this picture can be seen the White Catholic Church of Italian design named 'Our Lady of Peace'. This church, the gift of the Honourable Mrs. Fflorens Roch had its foundation stone laid in 1939 and was completed in 1940.

76. A view looking down High Street probably from the 1940s and there are a few familiar buildings to recall. On the left are Lloyds and Barclays banks and on the opposite side, Wallace Jones, Tabernacle church and Briggs shoe shop. On the bottom right is Andrew Thomas the newsagents which, as such, is run these days by the Hughes family.

77. From an early picture postcard this view is described as 'Newbridge From The Mountain', again giving a clear sight of the distant landscape where the building of the Pantside Estate has yet to begin.

78. Station Square with the corner shop of Morgans the fishmonger on the left. At the bottom was the former railway station which served passengers on the Great Western Region lines from Newport until the Spring of 1962.

79. Another important grocery chain of shops in a number of valley towns was Jones and Porter. Seen here in the early 1950s, are some members of staff of the Newbridge branch amongst whom are Moira Hawkins, Terry Shepherd, Pat Langley, Mary Jones, Barbara Watts, Des Pope, Enid Wilks, Norma Caleb, Edna Nash, Blanche Phillips and Ruth Daunter.

80. Celynen North Colliery, which began production of coal in 1916 when demand was at a peak in the midst of World War One. This picture however dates from the 1980s following the pit's closure.

81. The familiar blackened faces of miners are seen no more in the valleys. The gentleman pictured here in full working attire is the late Mr. John Freeman who worked at Celynen Colliery, following in the footsteps of his father, which tended to be a tradition in the mining industry. John would have been better known by his nickname 'Hot Dog'.

82. A more industrious scene at Celynen North and Graig Fawr. Graig Fawr was opened in 1924 and coal was raised there until closure in 1961. The three shafts showing from left to right are Graig Fawr, Box Pit and North Pit. The first manager of the Celynen North was Mr. J.M. Wallace and 14 year old Stan Medcraft was the first boy down the colliery.

83. Celynen Terrace, originally a row of forty-five houses built to accommodate shaft sinkers at the South Colliery in 1881. These were fine and typical examples of Welsh mineworkers' dwellings in every sense of the word, earning themselves the nickname 'Tub and Bucket Row'. This was attributed to the square stone slabs, almost three feet high which were placed outside and intended to hold old-fashioned wash tubs, a once-familiar sight. Celynen Row was almost a community in itself, the inhabitants voicing much protest when Abercarn Council served demolition orders and launched a re-housing programme in 1968.

84. The children of Celynen Row pose for a picture during the 1930s. Back: Kathleen Pugh, Nancy Pugh, Marion Clift, Monica Madden, Herbie Bull, Bryn Salisbury, Ray Box, Charlie McWilliam, Dennis Madden, Granville Madden and Betty Garbutt. Middle: Stan Pugh, Peggy Roberts, Billy Clift, John Clift, Bryn Box, Ivor Roberts and Tom Madden (with ball). Front: Jack Williams, Douglas Garbutt, Ronnie Owens and Billy Williams.

85. The year 1984 was probably the beginning of the end of the British coal industry. A national strike was called in March of that year and the dispute did not end until March 1985. The decision to close Celynen South had already been taken and despite a number of men being offered jobs at neighbouring pits still operating, some 75% of Celynen's workforce decided enough was enough and left the industry forever. The above picture from the colliery in 1984 was to become an all too familiar sight.

53

86. A view looking towards the former G.W.R. station at Newbridge, the original line from Newport being built by the Monmouthshire Canal and Railway Company. The first train arrived from Newport on Monday December 10th 1850 to be greeted by enthusiastic crowds who marvelled at this new-found means of passenger transport.

87. A team of gangers pause for a moment on the line just outside the station in the 1920s perhaps. When the line first opened in 1850, there was a strict ten miles per hour speed limit imposed by Act of Parliament. Steam trains gave way to diesel units in the 1950s but not for long, as the infamous 'Dr. Beeching axe' fell on the valley's passenger services in April 1962 and so ended more than a century of service.

88. A train passes through Celynen South Halt from the direction of Newbridge. The Halt which was primarily intended for use by colliery workers rather than passenger trains, was opened in 1933.

89. A photograph that typifies road transport in the Newbridge area at the turn of the last century. The local gentleman is a Mr. Lander and he is pictured near the South Celynen colliery whilst possibly on a coal delivery round.

90. The large building in the bottom left is the Celynen Collieries Workingmen's Institute which was built in 1907. This building was added to in 1924 and called the Memorial Hall (more widely known as The Memo), a popular dance hall and cinema. On the right is Zion Chapel and the apparent waste ground in the centre was used for the building of St. Paul's church in 1928.

91. The Celynen South Colliery, a mining operation that was started as early as 1873 by the Newport and Abercarn Black Vein Steam Coal Company. Three shafts were sunk here, two for winding the coal and one for essential ventilation purposes. The picture here is from around the 1930s and shows the buildings that housed the steam engines used to operate the winding system.

92. Workers are pictured having just returned to the surface at Celynen South and handing in their tags to Mr. John Roberts.

93. Four local colliers take a breather and a final cigarette before starting a shift underground at Celynen South in 1985. The gentlemen are, left to right Ted Grainger, Jack Thomas, Chris Smith and Eddie Speede. In its heyday Celynen employed almost 2000 men producing some 10,000 tons of coal per week.

94. A working headframe at Celynen through which coal was first raised in 1876, some three years after sinking commenced. The shafts reached a depth approaching 1200 feet, with some of the coal-working faces almost three miles from pit bottom.

CHAPTER 5

Religion & Schooling in Newbridge

95. The banner is held high by members of Beulah Sunday School as they march up High Street during a traditional Whitsun parade in the 1950s.

96. Hafod Fach (Small Summer House or Dwelling) the one-time home of John and Rachel Morgan. This was the birthplace of Baptist worship in Newbridge in the very early 1800s, inspired by the farmer's wife Rachel, who had despaired of her husband's conversion to the evil drink. Services were held regularly at Hafod Fach with the assistance of Rev. John Evans of Pontypool, all this leading to the eventual building of Beulah Chapel in 1810.

97. Some familiar faces perhaps in full song taking part in a once-popular round the town chapel parade in the 1950s.

98. The Welsh Baptist Chapel of Beulah, an ancient house of worship in Newbridge. Whilst still nothing more than a sparsely populated district in the year 1809, a large plot of land near the River Ebbw was leased for a period of 999 years from a Mr. Henry Symmonds, for the purpose of erecting a place of worship and Christian burial. Thus it was, that Beulah was opened for worship in the summer of 1810 much to the delight of the faithful Rachel Morgan and her followers. Noticeable on the side of the chapel and pavement are a number of steps; these were built to allow olden-day horse riders and passengers to dismount here.

99. A gathering of Ministers at Beulah Welsh Baptist Chapel in September 1960 comprises of the following gentlemen, left to right. Rev. T.J. Michael, Rev. R. Menai Jones, Rev. Glyndwr Richards and Rev. D.J. Davies.

100. A scene inside Beulah Chapel during a Whitsun tea party. A couple of young faces to spot include Jacqueline Roberts, Carol Nicholas, Roger Haines, Colin Roberts, Christopher Watkins and Derek Watkins.

101. Three leaders of a Beulah Chapel march in 1935 are Mr. Thomas James and Mr. Ambrose James (deacons) and in the centre Reverend Menai Jones.

102. Another enjoyable tea party is in progress at Beulah with plenty of faces for locals to identify.

103. Tabernacle English Baptist Church which has been in Newbridge for more than 140 years. Brimming with migrant workers from Hereford, Gloucester and the West Country, Newbridge in the mid nineteenth century, could only offer the Welsh tongue in its places of worship. By 1862 however, the English had firmly asserted their presence by building their own chapel, Tabernacle, which could house 300 worshippers. The building seen in this photograph however is the completely rebuilt church, which was opened in July 1913 and still stands today.

104. Pausing for a moment for a photograph during the 1940s are leaders of a march by members of Tabernacle Chapel. In the front are Reverend Hywel Morgan, Mr. John Edmunds and Mr. M. Coles. Just in the background on the right is Mr. Charles Harris.

105. The Gothic-styled St. Paul's Church which is built chiefly of local stone quarried at nearby Abercarn. The building seen here was opened for worship in 1929, replacing an original St. Paul's which was constructed of iron and opened in Church Road in the year 1889.

106. Many members of St. Paul's Sunday School are ready for a march around Newbridge in the 1950s. They are assembled near the Greystone buildings which may be remembered as being site of the doctors surgery a few years ago.

107. The former Greenfield School at Newbridge which was opened by the Mynyddislwyn School Board in 1876. Industrial expansion in the area soon saw a population explosion and one report by the school inspectorate recorded a class of 76 boys under the tutorship of just one teacher, in a classroom designed for a mere thirty! However it was not until 1921 that the overcrowding problems were properly dealt with, by the building of a completely new school which was to become known as Newbridge Grammar.

108. The staff of Greenfield School pictured in about 1962. Left to right they are - Back: Chris Padfield, M. Organ, Conrad Rees, Ralph Robinson, Terry Pike, Jen Schaffer and Will Griffiths. Third Row: Dorothy Davies, Rona Lewis, Ann Thomas, Mrs. Herbert, Glenys Doughty, Betty Stone, Maureen Pike and Beryl Jenkins. Second Row: Derek Morgan, Jack Price, Arthur Harris, Cecil Caffull, John Herbert, Norman Jones and Bill Gwynne. Front: Betty Marsh, Gwen Bowen, Gordon Groves (Headmaster), May Anstis and Jess Dugmore.

109. With shield and cup, is a victorious-looking team from Greenfield Secondary Modern A.F.C. in 1957. On the far left is Mr. Gordon Groves with fellow teacher Norman Jones on the right. The players are - Back: Michael Pook, John Presley, Colin Price, Gordon Jones, Brian Selway and Colin Gregory. Front: Lyndon Savigar, Robert Collins, Ron Self, Ken Pople and Bryan Davies.

110. The year is 1956 and a Greenfield School trip to Ireland is about to set off from Newport station. Amongst staff and pupils are Gordon Groves, Arthur Harris, Margaret Lawrence, Patricia Smith, Maria Worley, John Jenkins, John Davies, Graham Parker, Brian Craddick, Charlie Burgwin, John Blanche, John Gregory, Esmond Holley, Peter Powell, Ron Salmon, Alan Breeze, Dennis Hodges, David Owen, Russell Shipp, John Evans, Ken Mathuen, Colin Gregory, Francis Hillier and Abner Bates.

111. A picture taken in the school yard at Greenfield in the 1930s. It has not been possible to trace many names unfortunately but amongst those included are teacher Mr. Meller with two boys in the back, Horace Thomas and Arthur Griffiths. Some of the girls are Sylvia Woodman, Nancy English, Iris Mangol, Gladys Bennett, Mary Grubb with her sister and Maisie Thomas.

112. A young rugby team from Greenfield during the 1972 season with P.E. teacher Mr. Prior in the centre. The boys are - Back: David Case, Gary Holland, Adrian Niblett, Brian Harris, Philip Oxford, Kevin Andrews, Christopher Storey and David Hooper. Middle: Lyndon Phillips, Colin Rodwell, Steven Gardener, Andrew Davies, Keith Jenkins and Gary Sayce. Front: David Draper, Neil Williams and Philip Newman.

113. The teaching staff at Greenfield School in 1975 and they will be remembered as - Back: Keith Starr, Andrew Clark, Robert James, Peter Madden, Terry Pike, Bill Gwynne, Michael Matthews, Wynford Prior, Norman West, Colin Vickers and Robert Ashmead. Seated: Shirley Turner, Mary Jones, Arlene Tanner, Arthur Harris, Beryl Jenkins, John Herbert, Betty Marsh, Jack Price, Ethel Herbert, Tessa Williams and Pauline Foot.

114. A small party of children from Greenfield who are pictured during one of their visits to Hilston Park House Skenfrith. This was a popular old mansion house used as an outward bound centre by local schools. The pupils seen here are - Back: Michael Belt, Elaine Hopes, David Evans and David Owens. Front: Pamela Wallace, Linda Halfpenny, David Taylor and Wayne Kinsey.

115. Newbridge Comprehensive School pictured shortly after opening in 1921 when it was established as the town's Grammar School.

116. A 70 year-old view which shows the Welfare Bowling Green with the Grammar School, as it then was, in the background. Government legislation introduced in the 1970s, sought a fairer system of secondary education abandoning the so-called 'Eleven Plus' examination and replacing the term Grammar with Comprehensive.

117. The teaching staff of Tynewydd School in the 1920s. Second from the left in the front row is Miss Jane Hughes who was a well known teacher in Newbridge for some 43 years. Known locally as Miss Jenny, this senior citizen of the town celebrated her 100th birthday in 1998.

118. Another 1920s school photograph from Tynewydd and this time it is of Class VIa with Miss Freeguard the teacher on the far right. One pupil clearly identified is Mr. Reg Jones (Spoons) who is in the back row, second from the right.

119. This classroom photograph was taken at Tynewydd School in the mid 1960s, therefore some now 'adult' readers of this book may recognise a few pupils such as Theresa Phillips, Kim Evans, Catherine Madden, Susan Walters, Linda Halfpenny, Mike Jones, Anita Hawkesworth, Kim Walker, Ellen Bennett, Terry Price, Lynn Popel and Mark Gomoluch.

120. Tynewydd Junior School in 1954 with headmaster Mr. Jenkins on the right and Mrs. Weeks on the left. Not many pupils' names have come to light but here are a few to recall - Peter Cox, Victor Bloodworth, Bruce Barrowman, Brian Thomas, Ann Ward, Ruth Williams, Yvonne Saunders, Emanuella Davies, Jennifer Clarke, Margaret Herbert and Irene Herbert.

121. A girls' class is pictured at Tynewydd in about 1929 and a few pupils can be named, reading left to right. Front: Mary Parfitt (2nd), Edith Dyke (4th), Emily Ross (7th). Second Row: Lilian Jenkins, Elaine Salmon, Elaine Parry (6th, 7th, 8th). Third Row: Olga Wheeler, Abby Price, Phyllis Williams (1st, 2nd, 3rd), Marion Parsons (7th), Miss Thomas (Teacher, 9th). Back: Betty Clifford (2nd), Iris Lurvey (4th), Vera Edwards (7th).

122. This is how a classroom scene at Pentwynmawr School appeared in the year 1910. However, the scene is re-enacted to perfection nearly 90 years on by local pupils and teachers whilst visiting The Museum Of Welsh Life in Cardiff and careful study of the faces will reveal all. The four teachers are Marion Tamplin, Lynda Keeling, Mr. Hanlan and Lisa Sterry. Starting at the back the children include Lyndsey Stewart, Hayley Phillips, Leigh Powell, Amy Lloyd, Katie James, Dale Taylor, Christopher Mills, Michael East, Amy Hawkesford, Kate Storey, Carly Williamson, Carly Smith, Adam Roberts, Simon Gardener, James Lapping, Rachel Trinder, Jonathan Nowaczyk, Richard Davies, Rachel Johnson, Adam Churchill, Ben Brotherwood, Andrew Prettyjohns and Christopher Williams.

123./124. Both of these photographs were taken at Pentwynmawr Council Mixed School in 1921 and show pupils and teachers from Standards 2 and 3. Any surviving children would now be well into their 'eighties' yet hopefully also, there is a grandparent or parent to be recognised somewhere in the pictures.

125. The mixed scholars with their teachers at Pentwynmawr School. The school here first opened in 1908 catering for just fifty pupils but by 1912, it had been considerably extended to accommodate 250.

CHAPTER 6

Sport, Entertainment & Newbridge people

126. Newbridge boy Paul Turner pictured with his first Welsh Rugby Cap which was well-earned in 1989.

The highly respected Newbridge Rugby Club was founded in the year 1888, literally playing on any vacant local field in the beginning. One favourite spot for a number of years was Top Flats, an area which nowadays is occupied by the Treowen Housing Estate. One 'not so favourite pitch' was Waen Bedr (Useless Ground) which many a visiting side particularly complained that it had an absurd gradient of one in four! Eventually in 1921 the club settled in the more familiar Welfare Ground, wasteland which had been purchased by a local colliery company. Hard economic times delayed development somewhat and it was 1926 before the ground was fully completed, much of the work being carried out by local out-of-work miners. The prevailing poverty of the period was well illustrated by the fact that the men were quite prepared to offer their labour for a bowl of soup and a cigarette, which were provided by the Newbridge Welfare Association. Progress in the world of rugby was relatively slow until the 1940s, when at last Newbridge gained recognition as a first-class club by gaining its first international player with Billy Gore in the 1946-47 season. The successes thereafter require more space than this book can provide and thus, should there be a second volume, the history will be continued in fine detail.

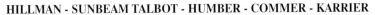

127. The Youth Players at Newbridge in the 1963-64 season and left to right are - Back: Don Waite, Binky Williams (Committee), Geoff Williams, Stuart Mills, Gordon Shipp, Alan Davies, David Davies, Ralph Thomas, ?, Jack Shepperd and Jim Caddick (Committee). Middle: Graham Shipp, Richard Hodges, John Davies (Captain), David Finch and Jeff Norman. Front: Jeff Rogers, Terry Evans, Peter Peacock, Jeff Thomas, Peter Hoare and David Friend.

128. The Bowls Club at Newbridge has quite a long history, it having been formed in about 1924. This picture however is from the mid 1980s with a host of players as follows, from left to right. Back: Ray Preece, Ron Benstead, Don Jones, Colin White, Clive Wilkes, Steve Beach, Jack Vowles, Dennis Edwards, Neil Tyler, Alan Rogers, Chris Jones, Eddie Lewis and Harry Elley. Middle: Ron Jones, Gary Williams, Jim Prosser, Eddie Potts, Robert Bishop, Gwynne Leonard, John Bullock, Gordon Wilson, Jim Jackson, Ernie Hiley, John Lewis and Frank Pfeiffer. Front: Tom Cox, Bernard Millinship, Desmond Edge, John Herbert, John Tyler, Bill Chivers, Horace Beach, Norman Williams, Des Henry, Dennis Wigg and Percy Hawkins.

129. Another example of sporting stardom to emanate from Newbridge is Wales' professional snooker player Lee Walker, seen here in 1998 amidst a collection of cups and trophies.

130. Before being superseded by snooker, billiards was a favourite pastime in many local clubs and institutes. Here are the highly successful players of the Celynen Collieries Institute in 1914. Back: W. Williams, A. Evans, W. Wilson, E.T. Jones, T.J. Davies, J. Lilley and T. Wrighton. Fourth Row: E.P. Stephens, B. Morris, C. Powell, L. Burnett, M.H. Badge, C. Meek, L. Hughes and F.G. Salter. Third Row: W. Williams, D. Jones, E. Smith, Dr. T.A. Gregg, M. Pugh, T. Hadwell and G. Richards. Front: A. Wooley and S. Coleman. Inset: C. Hopkins.

131. A young man whose life was tragically cut short was Richard Davies of Pentwynmawr, son of Hayden and Trudy. A pupil of Newbridge Comprehensive School, 'Ritchie' is seen here with his hero, Ryan Giggs a star of Manchester United Football Club.

132. A First XI Football Team belonging to Pentwynmawr School from many seasons ago. Again, there may well be a reader of this book who will recognise a boy or two?

133. The Treowen Stars A.F.C. with a trophy during the 1971-72 season. Left to right are - Back: John Charles, Mike Young, Robert Davies, Robert Higgins, David Wilcox and Archie Davies. Front: Philip Walker, Kelvin Thorn, Alan Parfitt, David Bevan, Glyn Francis and Alan Beacham. The mascot on this occasion is a young Andrew Bevan.

134. These young girls after their last year in the Pant Side School moved on to Newbridge Comprehensive School, once the Grammar School. This picture from 1986-87 shows Back - Mrs. Jennifer Rowlands, Michelle Hughes, Louise Cheshire, Caroline Watts and Rachel Arlin. Front - Emma Spear, Nicola Tudor, Leanne Smart, Kelly Burgess and Lindsey Jones.

135. The Rugby XV at Greenfield School during a successful 1957-58 season. Back row: Dennis Hodges, Charles Burgwin, Alan Breese, Russell Shipp, Brian Twinburrow and Barry Mills. Middle: Raymond Beecham, Alan Mainwaring, Peter Powell (Captain), John Jenkins and Roger Morgan. Front: Graham Parker, Gerald Gamson, Keith Davies and Wayne Protheroe.

136. The presentation of a shield is in progress to members of the Newbridge Judo Club during the early 1950s and a few names from the past are as follows - Tommy Garland, Leighton Jenkins, Terry Edmunds, Larry Evans, Molly Hicks, Barry Webb, Lyndon Irwyn and Sheila Smith.

137. Newbridge boxer Joe Calzaghe, trained by his father Enzo, won the A.B.A. Champion 3 times before moving on to win the British Super-Middleweight title. But the biggest night of his career so far was in October 1997 when he won the W.B.O. World Super-Middleweight title by defeating Chris Eubank.

138. Selwyn Evans another product of Newbridge Boxing Club. He turned professional in 1947 and was reigning light-weight Champion of Wales 1950 to 1953.

139. Newbridge Boxing Club opened in 1940 over Wallace Jones' shop in Newbridge. Fred Taylor was the Secretary with Wyndham Price and Edgar Parry the trainers. Early in 1946 the club moved to the welfare boxing gym in Newbridge where it still stands today. One of the earliest successes to come out of the gym was Jimmy Roberts (inset) who in 1945 along with Selwyn Evans represented Wales in matches against Denmark and Sweden, being the first boxing team to tour after the end of the War. Roberts, originally from old Treowen, turned professional around 1949-50. He went on to win the Welsh Middleweight title in 1951 and later lost this title to Roy Hagland at Abergavenny. This was his last fight before he retired.

140. A picture from the distant past during inclement weather at Newbridge in the year 1912. With the horse and cart at North Road is the local road sweeper and maintenance man employed at the time Mr. Oliver Lovell on the left, with Ellis Lovell in the cart. Unfortunately it has not been possible to trace the name of the assistant on the right.

141. No mining town would dream of being without a brass or silver band in years gone by and here is the Celynen Band in 1960. In the back row are Roy Donovan, Terry Hawkins, Ron Probyn, Ken Haywood, Roger Freeman, Arthur Beale Snr., Robert Beale, Peter Jenkins, David Banwell, Bryn Elias Jnr., Howard Stone and Colin Price. Middle: David Roberts, Bryn Elias Snr., Sylvia Elias, Mr. West (North Colliery Manager), Irene Banwell, T. David Probyn (Conductor) and Tom Roberts. Front: Arthur Pitcher, Anthony Allan, Allain Probyn and Hayden Stredwick.

142. Another collection of young members of Celynen Band and here we see Bryn Elias, Peter Jenkins, Robert Beale, Roy Donovan, Peter Jenkins (Snr.), Peter Jenkins (Jnr.), David Roberts, Terry Hawkins, Roger Freeman, John Harris, Colin Price, David Banwell, Irene Banwell, Madelaine Wilson, Sylvia Elias, Ron Probyn, Allan Maddox, Ken Haywood, Philip Morgan, Arthur Pitcher, John Pidgeon, Hayden Stredwick, T. David Probyn (Conductor), Allain Probyn, Anthony Allan and Martin Jones.

143. The talents of Mr. Reg Jones are quite well known throughout the valley and beyond. Better known as 'Spoons', due to his unique form of entertainment with the utensils, he is seen here accompanied by a mascot goat at Newbridge Welfare Carnival in the 1970s.

144. June 2nd 1953 saw the coronation of Queen Elizabeth II with parties and carnivals being held across the country, albeit the weather did not live up to expectations. Here are some local girls at Fields Park, amongst whom are Christine Hodges, Linda Symonds, Irene Thomas, Gloria Keeling, Ann Morgan, Glenys Evans and Maureen Dyer.

145. A Pantside Carnival Float makes its way for judgement at Newbridge Welfare Ground in the mid 1960s. The topic is Old Time Music Hall and some of those aboard the wagon are Lil Morris (with cap), Margaret Cook (standing), Marion George, Evelyn Coombes, Doreen James, Leana Thomas (at the piano) and Margaret Williams (standing).

CHAPTER 7

Crumlin & Hafodyrnynys

146. A view of the square probably dating from the 1930s judging by the model of the lone motor car in the main street. The name Crumlin is said to be derived from 'Cromlech', a designation given to ancient Druidicial monuments. Until the latter years of the nineteenth century, Crumlin was a 'border town', the community finding itself located in two separate parishes, Llanhilleth and Mynyddislwyn.

147. The Square as it appears today, the whole area having been transformed. Growing up as it did during the industrialisation of the nineteenth century, the town lay in the heart of what was referred to as the South Wales Coal Basin. Consequently, local and neighbouring quarries became popular hunting grounds for a wide variety of ancient fossils from a prehistoric age.

148. A view of old Crumlin that was taken around 1905 with much of the scenery having changed beyond all recognition these days.

149. Crumlin Viaduct, which had stood as the valley's most outstanding monument to railway engineering for more than a hundred years. Officially opening on June 1st 1857, it had taken almost five years to complete from its original planning stage, and now provided vital and important rail links between Hereford, Pontypool, the western valleys and beyond.

150. The former Great Western Railway Low Level Station at Crumlin. Initially constructed by the Monmouthshire Railway and Canal Company, the line from Newport was opened for traffic in December 1850. Whilst the journey was probably far more comfortable than that offered by coach and horses, early timetables show that the trip from Newport to Crumlin still took some eighty minutes to complete!

151. A panoramic view across the Ebbw Valley from about 1918 and one notable feature is the absence of housing, which has yet to be built in the Swffryd area.

152. A picture of Crumlin in the 1950s with the viaduct still intact. The last train crossed the viaduct on June 13th 1964 and shortly afterwards, Hollywood stars Sophia Loren and Gregory Peck were guests in the area for filming of the adventure movie *'Arabesque'* which featured Crumlin's famous bridge.

153. The High Level Station at Crumlin which was opened in 1857 and closed in June 1964, following the withdrawal of passenger services between Pontypool and Aberdare. The station sign indicates 'Change for Western Valley' which of course meant that passengers on their journey to nearby Llanhilleth for instance, faced a substantial walk with their luggage down the hill to the Low Level Station as seen in photograph number 150.

154. A view of Crumlin's town centre to remind readers of a not-to-distant past. On the left is Bank House and on the right may be seen the Italian Cafe, Walls Ironmongers, The Ex-Servicemen's Club and Pugsleys Butcher's Shop.

155. Another scene from the centre showing the Navigation Miners' Institute on the left and the Empire Buildings on the right.

156. A one-time centrepiece of The Square was the Railway Hotel which is seen here in the 1930s. To the right of the hotel, some readers may remember Humes General Store and to the left, a hairdressing shop.

157. In the early years of the twentieth century Crumlin was blessed with two Baptist chapels namely, Noddfa in Kendon Road and Jerusalem in Hafodyrynys Road. In about 1919, both churches united at Jerusalem and re-named it Bethel which is seen in the above photograph.

158. The Navigation Colliery with its two shafts was another former landmark in Crumlin. The colliery was opened by the Partridge Jones Company in 1911 and coal was mined here until 1968. Visitors to this part of the Ebbw Valley, will still be able to see some remaining brick-built buildings belonging to the Navigation which stand to the side of the main road through Crumlin.

159. A view of the viaduct which also shows the former brewery belonging to local man, David Francis Pritchard who operated in Viaduct Road. It was a member of his family who went on to design a famous trademark which was to be recognised throughout the licensed trade for many years - the 'Hobby Horse'. This was adopted by the Rhymney and Crosswell Company and was to be seen decorating the walls of many a public house in South Wales.

160. A photograph taken from one of the last passenger trains to cross the viaduct. The scene, some 200 feet below, has been totally transformed with new roadways and bridges in recent years. The viaduct originally carried two rail tracks thus allowing trains to pass at once, however as the years went by, increased and much heavier traffic than was first planned for, brought questions of structural safety and as to whether the 70 year-old foundations were beginning to crumble; this being understandable considering the proximity of underground coal workings. Thus in 1928 it was decided to reduce the crossing to single-line traffic and also impose a new speed limit of 8 miles per hour.

161. Crumlin Boys Club 1938-39. Pictured from left to right are - Back: Ernie Hughes, Ken Magnus, Glyn Nash, Wilf Gingel, Bert Shipp, Len Avon and Tom Holland. Middle: Bill Jones, Cyril Williams, Billy Hughes, John Tucker and Glyn Horseman. Front: Ron Harris, Glyn Morgan and Alban Daley.

162. Members of a victorious Under 15s rugby team from Crumlin who were tournament winners during a tour of Italy in 1993 and left to right are: Back: Lawson Jones, Chris Sheldon, Dean Andrews, Lee Llewellyn, Dean Gibbs, Mark Curtis, Ian Carpenter, James Scott, Lewis Hamer, Sam Brewster, Gareth Gleadall, Ross Hewlett and Gary Hewlett. Front: Lee Jones, Greg Davies, Tom Llewellyn, Matthew Williams (Captain), Steve Thomas, Chris Lewis, Jonathan Williams and Martin Gleadall.

163. The 'New' Council Schools Crumlin pictured here shortly after opening in 1912. The original school was in Crown Street and opened in 1885 by the Mynyddislwyn School Board.

164. Some members of staff at Crumlin High Level School during the 1970s and they include - Back: Ken James, Sheila Wellington, unknown, unknown and Michael Tiley. Front: William Marsh, John Taylor and Maureen Pike.

165. Teacher Sylvia Hill is seen at the school in about 1968 with a class, most of whom can be remembered as follows - Back: Steven Shipp, Neil Green, Alan Stinton, Leighton Frayne, ?, Andrew Barratt, Philip Holly and Andrew Davies. Middle: M. Smith, Keith Beddis, Julie Shallish, Jenny Clissett, Gail Fricker, Paul Hopkins, ? and Martin Simmons. Front: Angela Hinch, Nigel Wallace, Debbie Haford, Glynys Hobdon, Brian Bourne, Elizabeth Reed, Kim Cotterell and unknown.

166. The year is believed to be 1968 and here are some more pupils under the watchful eye of Mrs. Pike. Back: Alan Bourne, ?, Tracey Barrett, Angela Davies, Theresa Potts, Shirley Richards, Jill Whitcombe, Andrew Gingell, Neil Jones and Beth Vowles. Third Row: Anne-Marie Sandall, Janet Dundon, Athleen Bourne, Sian Hayden, Ian Ackerman, Michael Cottle, Karen Burnett, Neil Hallett and Daryl Palmer. Second Row: Jacqueline Davies, Julie Allaway, Beverley Hopkins, Sian Turner, Sian Hughes, Julie Chess, Jane Leonard, Catherine Reader, Susan Williams, Denise Gaida and Frances Williams. Front: Leighton Powell, Stuart Hughes, David Blanche, Andrew Dugmore, David Homer, Michael Jones, Arthur Otter, Colin Erasmus and Stuart Shepherd.

167. A classroom of Crumlin High Level School 1898 is re-enacted in this picture taken at St. Fagan's Museum and the following pupils and staff are seen. Mr. Tilley (Head) and Mrs. Philpots (Teacher) with pupils Sammy Jo Smithy, Rachael Roberts, Michael Hadigate, Cassie Leigh, Joel Andrews, Christopher Thomas, Thomas Andrews, Jamie Johnson, Lloyd Penn, Joel Mock, Michaela ?, Rebecca James, Sarah Lou Petrie, Michelle Stinchcombe, Shauna Hopkins, Bethany Phelps, Sam Andrews, Rhys Bennett, Hayley Davies, Emily Gait, Kira Walker, Rachael Davies, Adam ?, Nicky Givens, Connor Guest and Joshua Sterry.

168. The Hafodyrynys Hotel as it appeared a few years ago, during times when it was possible to buy petrol as well as alcoholic refreshment here.

169. A scene at Hafodyrynys in the 1950s when coal was king. Whilst there was a small undertaking here in the 1880s, it was not until the outbreak of war in 1914 that the colliery was properly developed. At the time of this photograph, Hafodyrynys was linked to neighbouring pits at Glyntillery and Tirpentwys; the links also being used in later years to transport coal underground from Blaensychan to Glyntillery. Hafodyrynys ceased production in September 1966 and the workings seen here, now form the site of a busy road to Pontypool.

170. Modern-day residents may find it difficult to imagine that there ever was railway service in Hafodyrynys. However here is the proof required, as a train from Pontypool pulls into the wooden-platformed halt in the late 1950s; opened in 1913, closure finally came in June 1964 together with Crumlin viaduct.

171. Hafodyrynys Sports Committee members are seen at the Welfare Club in the 1960s having celebrated a rugby presentation cup to John Griffiths. In the picture are - Back: Will Jones, Ivor Loud, Spencer Jayne, Colwyn Tovey and Ken Stone. Front: Will Jones, Bryn Roberts, John Griffiths, Leslie Drew and Hayden Jenkins.

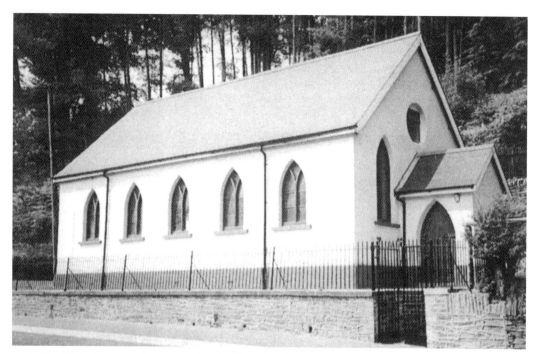

172. Hafodyrynys Congregational Church which was built as a daughter church of Capel-yr-Ynys, Cefn-y-Crib in 1895.

173. Above is Mrs. Dorothy Davies who is seen cutting the cake during her 100th birthday celebrations that were held at the Hafodyrynys Congregational Church. Mrs. Davies lived in Herbert Street and passed away in November 1999 shortly before her 103rd birthday.

174. Some faithful ladies of the church pictured during the Harvest Festival celebrations of 1995 and they are - Back: Pat Lewis, Glenys Lewis, Hazel Davies, Venus Challenger, Elizabeth Lewis and Gwynneth Smith. Front: Dorothy Davies and Ada Lovell.

175. A proud moment for members of Hafodyrynys Sunday School as they display the Pontypool and District Scripture Examination shield in 1952. Left to right they are - Back: Colwyn Tovey, William Knight and George Lovell. Middle: Anita Jenkins, Betty Pritchard, David Webb, Gary Summers, Barry Price, Marion Loud, Elaine Pritchard and Ada Lovell. Front: Clive Goff, Anthea Durbin, Eileen Johns, Jean Ford, Meryl Jenkins, Janice Hewlett, Ann Loud and Alan Tovey.

176. Going back some years, on this occasion to 1927, when the village of Hafodyrynys produced a much acclaimed juvenile choir. This photograph shows the accompanist Gwyneth Tovey and conductor William Jenkins surrounded by an impressive shield and collection of trophies.

177. From the year 1927 the Hafodyrynys Junior Choir is pictured with a trophy and many names are known and numbered as follows, seen left to right - Front: Gwen Davies, Margaret Jones, Gwyneth Tovey - Pianist, William Jenkins - Conductor (Nos. 3, 4, 6, 7). Second Row: Annie Edwards, Fred Morgan, Ms. Jory, Ivor Challenger, Jack Ford, Horace Rees (Nos. 1, 9, 10, 11, 12, 13). Third Row: L. Llewellyn, Bill Jones, Ralph James, Gerald Jones, Harry Rees, Fred Edwards, Jack Davies, Jack Downes, Lily Tovey (Nos. 9 to 17). Fourth Row: William Jones (Bon Pren), Agnes Woods, Linda Jenkins, Agnes Price (Nos. 1, 4, 5, 17). Back: Miss Walker, Ethel Griffiths, Dolly Wilkinson, Richard Griffiths, Emlyn Jenkins, Wilf Price, Richard Edwards, Henry Jenkins (Nos. 1, 7, 9, and 14 to 18).

178. A scarce surviving picture of Hafodyrynys School taken in about 1910. The school opened in January 1901 to cater for an increasing number of village pupils who previously, had to travel to school at Pantygasseg. Hafodyrynys School closed in 1985, later to be demolished and since replaced by housing. The last head teacher may be remembered by former pupils as Mr. Clive Holyfield.

179. Members of staff at the school during the 1920s but unfortunately only three can now be identified. Left back is Miss Phyllis Lewis, left front Mrs. Jones with Mr. Hagstorm in the centre.

180. A traditional school photograph circa. 1918 of Group IV with teacher Mr. Hagstorm in attendance. Just a few names have become available on this occasion as follows - Back: Dillys Johns and Margaret Fiddy (6th and 7th). Third Row: Rhoda Brown (5th). Second Row: Tommy Dutton (far right). Front: Tom James (3rd) and Mervyn Thomas (6th).

181. The Junior School in about 1951 with teachers Miss Maydon left and Lilian Jones right. Amongst the pupils identified are - Back: Alan Woods, Barry Price and Terry Pearce (Nos 3, 4 and 5). Middle: Alan Tovey, Malcolm Pike, Janice Hewlett, ?, Anthea Durbin, Rhys Rees, Vera Jones and David Webb. Front: Clive Goff, Jean Ford, Marilyn Saunders, ?, Jenny Randell, Ann Loud, Meryl Jenkins, Eryl James and Glyndwr Jones.

182. This photograph taken at the end house of Herbert Street shows an early class from the school with teachers Nellie Jones on the left and Miss Swantun the right. The girls nearest the centre right include Ada Brown, Gladys Price, Rene Brown and Millie Davies. The boy on the far left in the middle row is Ivor Rosser.

183. This is Group 3 at the school in 1922 according to the slate the little girl is holding in the centre of the picture. In the front are Jack Davies, Jim Brown and Cliff Webb who are numbers 4, 5, 6 from the left. Second row numbers 1 and 3 are Billy Morgan and Linda Jenkins.

184. Another school photograph from Hafodyrynys in about 1950 and many of the girls can be identified - Back: Cherith James, Janice Hewlett, Eileen Johns, Vera Jones, ?, Marilyn Saunders and Barbara Cook. Middle: Anne Morris, June Webb, Dawn Rees, Meryl Jenkins, ?, Eira Price and Jean Ford. Front: Sonia Jones, ? , Diane Tovey, Diane Randal and Joan Venn.

CHAPTER 8

Abercarn & Cwmcarn

185. Abercarn 'bottom' Post Office which was in Bridge Street. Before being converted into a Post Office, the premises belonged to Mr. Edgar Meredith the popular local barber. Some Post Office staff whose names may be familiar include Mrs. Mary Butler who ran the business for ten years until 1978 assisted by Mrs. Haywood and Mrs. Williams.

186. A 'Bird's Eye View' of Abercarn from about 1920. The view includes the hills of Mynyddislwyn, a popular venue for sheep dog trials with the tin works in the lower left. In the lower right was the site of the Abercarn blast furnace, which was operating in the year 1782 and owned by the Glovers of Birmingham. The works were sold in 1808, to Richard Crawshay who subsequently passed the Abercarn Estate on to his son-in-law Benjamin Hall the second. The site of the furnace later became No.1 pit shaft and eventually these days, is occupied by a builders' yard.

187. The two prominent buildings seen here have since been demolished but will no doubt be remembered by many. On the left was the Workingmen's Institute and Library and in the centre are the offices belonging to the old Abercarn Urban District Council; these offices were pulled down in 1979.

188. Here are perfect examples of early Welsh industrial valley housing - The Ranks which were built by the Abercarn and Gwyddon Colliery Company for their workers in about 1850. A contemporary account described these company houses as *'two storeys high, having four lofty rooms with ceilings and fine flagstone ground floors with convenient fireplaces; outside is the privy, coal bunker and rubbish receptacle, ashes to be removed daily at the company's expense.'*

189. The ill-fated Prince Of Wales Colliery scene of the county's worst ever pit disaster in September 1878 when some 268 miners lost their lives in a massive underground explosion. The disaster left 138 widows and 364 children without fathers, with many of the men's bodies never to be recovered from beneath the ground.

190. Foxens Garage at Abercarn with Abercarn Tin Works to the back on the left of the picture.

191. A picture from the opening ceremony at the Korner Kitchen Cafe April 1987 and left to right are Councillor Bill Davies, Jan Price (proprietor) and Miss Emily Howard. This cafe was for many years known as 'Howards Cafe', the Howard family having come to Abercarn in 1940 and running the business until retirement in 1985.

192. This picture shows Howard's Cafe in Victoria Buildings at the lower end of the High Street. The cafe and sweet shop owned by the Howard's family did a vast amount of trade years ago with the children from Gwyddon School. The shop on the right at one time 'Griff Davies' is shown here as a builder's shop owned by Ted Price.

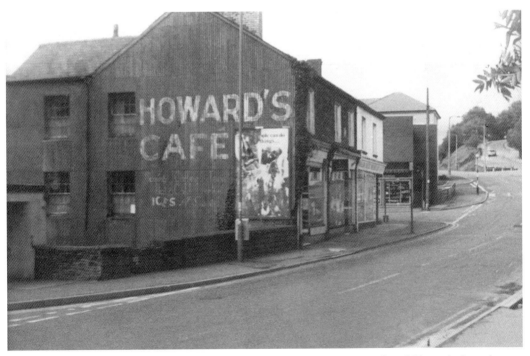

193. Another view of Howard's Cafe showing on the far left is the old bus shelter that was used for many years. Underneath the main road ran an old tram line from Abercarn Blast Furnace down to the old ironworks. The tunnel can still be seen by the side of the cafe building.

194. An aerial view of Abercarn that has changed somewhat since. There are numerous important buildings to recall such as the Library and Institute, the Welsh Church, which had opened in 1853 and the Council Offices. On the right, the ground locally known as the 'distillery' that once housed a bottle factory and close by was the 18th-century blast furnace. Also in the picture by the distillary pond is the old fair which came to this valley every year. In the front left are The Ranks, originally consisting of four rows of cottages. When this picture was taken sometime in the late 1960s or early 1970s two rows had already been demolished. The final two rows were also demolished in January 1983.

195. Abercarn Scout Group Committee from 1975. Back: Howell Price Stevens, Glyn Rees, Barbara Edwards, Andrea Price, Olive Rathbourne, ?, Pauline Jeenes, John Jeenes, Sylvia Dowden. Front: Mr. & Mrs. Burton, Mrs. Britt, Barbara Price Stevens, Reg Dowden, Margaret Harris, Kath Michael and Oliver Thorne.

196. This picture was taken at a Carnival at Abercarn. Unfortunately only one name has been traced and that is of Alec Edwards, the boy in the black jacket to the left of the ape. He went on to become leading fireman at Abercarn Fire Station.

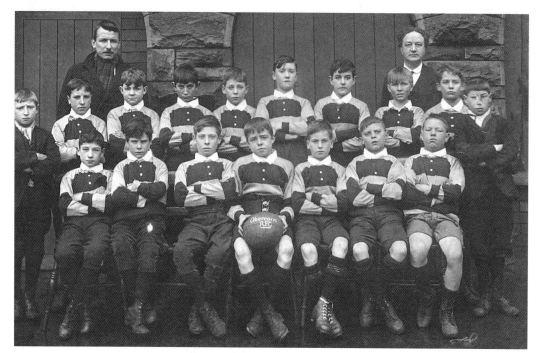

197. West End School Rugby Team taken around 1919-1920. Back: Trainer Josh Hide and Teacher Ted John. Standing: Arthur Coles, Len Russell, Pete Selby, 'Ginty' Adams, Fred Howells, Glyn Savage, ? Chick, Fred Fox, Patsy Grace, ? Madden. Seated: Stan George, Len Williams, Ted Lavender, John Hide, Cyril Jones, Dai Williams and 'Canon' Smith.

198. The Victoria Hall is seen here shortly before its demolition in 1971 to make way for a new by-pass road through the town. The Hall was opened in about 1902 and was a thriving attraction, staging travelling concerts and amateur dramatics. By the outbreak of war in 1914, 'silent films' were the new attraction, the 'talkies' arriving in 1929; it remained in use as a cinema until closure in 1945, eventually falling into a state of disrepair.

199. This picture shows the steel bridge over the Crumlin arm of the Monmouthshire Canal at the Chapel of Ease Abercarn. and in the background the High Meadow Housing Estate. This part of the canal opened in 1799 and through a distance of 11 miles it climbed through 32 locks. A reservoir was constructed at Cwmcarn to supply the water for the canal and in 1875 it burst its banks killing Mr. J. Hunt a flannel manufacturer and all his family. The Crumlin arm of the canal closed in 1949.

200. A photograph which might deliver a chill to some readers, an open-air swimming pool in Abercarn! During its time however, it was a popular venue and this picture shows the shop on the right, run by the Heath family of Pantside and the payment kiosk at the far end.

201./202. Two pictures which show the fire station at Abercarn and some of the men who served it. The station itself was built in 1924 and the picture below shows a presentation at the station in 1932 unfortunately, only a few of the men can be named. Back: Leading Fireman Alec Edwards and next to him his father Charles Edwards who both resided at the station. The gentleman presenting the cup is Mr. Morses and the recipient is Mr. Hicks.

203. This pony and cart scene at the top end of High Street, Abercarn shows Tom Reynolds (left) delivering milk in the 1920s. Tom lived with his brother Matt at Glanshon Farm until his marriage. The shop behind the cart was an outfitters shop owned and run by Mr. W. Jones of West End, Abercarn. Mr. Jones was locally known as 'Billy Ready Made'. Far left in this picture can also be seen The Garn Church.

204. From the railway line can be seen a good view of the 'Abercarn Tinworks' and the old village of Abercarn. This is how the scene appeared before the construction of the numerous modern buildings and factory units that now occupy this part of the valley.

205. Lady Llanover's Church, Abercarn known locally as the 'Welsh Church'. The church was built in 1853 for Benjamin Hall on his own estate. Mr. Hall who was a local landowner, M.P. and a Government Minister married his wife Augusta, who was better known as Lady Llanover in 1823. Although the couple were Anglicans they were extremely passionate for the Welsh language, so all services were held in Welsh. In 1859, Sir Benjamin Hall was made a peer and known as Baron Llanover of Llanover and Abercarn. He died in 1867 leaving a widow and a daughter. Lady Llanover seen in the inset above survived a further thirty years residing mainly at Llanover but maintaining a close connection with Abercarn.

206. Although not certain, it is thought that this scene is from the opening of the War Memorial in The Square, Abercarn. The participants cannot be named for obvious reasons but probably in attendance were quite a few Lords and dignitaries.

207. St. Lukes Church, Abercarn a citadel-like church with battlement tower. The foundation stone was laid on September 17th 1924 and it opened in March 1926. After the last service was taken here in Autumn 1983, it was hoped that perhaps it could be opened as a museum or a craft shop but nothing materialised and the church now lays in ruins. To the left of the picture are Polkers Cottages, now demolished.

208. A picture of the choir taken at the last service held at St. Lukes Church in Autumn 1983. Back: Organist Mrs. Coral Gibbs, Norman Hicks, Dean Rees, Bob Sloman, Edgar Garland and Roy Powell. Middle: Joyce Powell, Lucy Sloman, Nicola Price, Rev. Ray Summers, Ruth Avon, Pam Summers, Margaret Hicks and Olive Garland. Front: Martine Woodward, Emma Sumers, Jayne Harvey, Joanne Lewis, Joanne Peddle, Christianne Dugmore and Kayleigh Sloman.

209. This picture taken in High Street shows a great march being led from the old Iron Church West End, Abercarn to the opening of St. Lukes Church on Polker Hill in March 1926. The large building on the right was then the house of the tinplate works manager, it later becoming the Institute and is now Abercarn Rugby Club and a car park. In the background can be seen the shaft of The Prince of Wales Colliery which saw Gwent's worst pit disaster in 1878 with 268 miners losing their lives.

210. The Garn Congregational Church, Abercarn. Built on a 'parcel of land' leased by Lord Llanover in 1841 at a cost of £600. Services for the first twenty-one years were all in Welsh until 1862 when the transition from Welsh, to bi-lingual, to English was carried through under the guidance of a Rev. William Williams.

211. Abercarn Chapel and Cemetery. The first burial at the cemetery took place on 2nd February 1901 performed by Rees Davies the deceased being a one month old child named Victoria Mary Launders from Llanover Terrace, Cwmcarn. The chapel was built in 1900-1901 and the last service was held there in 1961.

212. A general view of West End Abercarn taken from the top of Abercarn Quarry in September 1982. In the centre is the Cae Gorlan Chapel and to its left the old West End Junior School.

213. Teaching Staff at West End School, Abercarn between 1915-1920. Some of the names have been traced and these are - Back: 2nd from left Ted Johns and 3rd from right Mrs. Anna Jane Thomas. Front: 3rd from left Miss Rosser, to her right Headmaster Mr. Jimmy Hughes, 6th from left Miss Richards and on the end Mrs. Rowlands, wife of Edward Rowlands. Mr. Rowlands and his father were both registrars in the old village of Abercarn many years ago.

214. West End School and School House, Abercarn. In 1970 it was announced that the school would be the first in Monmouthshire to be replaced under a government scheme for improving schools built before 1903. In fact West End possessed records dating back to before 1880. Many, later to become famous names appeared on the register of the old Abercarn West End School, among them Sir Clement Price Thomas, who was surgeon to King George VI.

215. A class from West End School, Abercarn taken around 1930. Back: ?, ?, Ivy Parker, Gwynneth Hall, ?, Dorothy Green and Betty Dawes. Middle: Terry Hicks, ?, ?, ?, Doreen Harris, Dora Fellstard, Betty Robinson, Irene Dawes, Jean Morgan, Rena Richards, Glenys Brooks, ?. Front: Nesta Emery (daughter of the Headmaster), Vera Dent, Rene Farr, Miss Rogers, Mavis Hill, Chris Joiner, Lorna Ridd, ?.

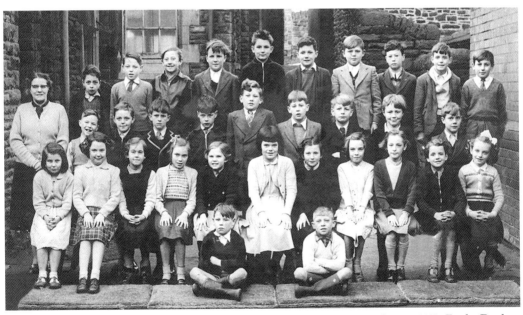

216. Another class from West End School, Abercarn this time from 1956. Back: Paul Tiley, John Derrick, Wayne Taylor, Colin Birt, Vernon Hughes, Dennis Chick, ?, David Williams, Tommy Redman, ?. Third row: Graham Way, ?, Keith Knight, John Maggs, Brian Lashbrook, Grayson White, Gareth Sainsbury, John Lewis, Derek Huish, ?. Second row: ?, Janet Purnell, Christine Allan, Beth Phillips, Carol Pugh, ?, Beth Price, Norma Wilcox, Christine Chess, Valerie Edmunds and Denise Haydon. Front: Robert Evans and Cyril Love.

217. Gwyddon Secondary Modern School 2nd VII Netball Team. Back: Mr. G. Parry, E. Smith, V. Hawkesford, K. Lewis, J. Tyrell and Mrs. G. Llewellyn. Front: A. Salisbury, C. Greenslade, S. Edwards (Captain), and P. Smith.

218. Form 1a Gwyddon Secondary Modern School, Abercarn 1955. Back: Jimmy Partridge, Donald Burrows, Malcolm Davies, Raymond Webb, Delwyn Short, John Clark, Robert Hart, Colin David, Clem Smith, Colin Edmunds, Granville Ryall, Brian Haines and teacher Mr. Miles. Middle: David Gibbons, Gerald Miles, Keith Summerhays, Roy Guy, Carol Sage, Julie Dugmore, Elaine Baldwin, Janice Redman, Kathleen Haines, Howell Williams, Cedric Noakes, Brinley Birt and Fred Bird. Front: June Staples, Zoya Butterworth, Pamela Smith, Jenny Davies, Barbara Parker, Janet Lawrence, Barbara Dodsworth, Patricia Badman, Barbara Burnett, Andrea Selby and Sylvia Townsend.

219. Cwmcarn Colliery began production in 1913 and was eventually closed by the National Coal Board in 1968. Today the site has been completely cleared and the land is part of the Cwmcarn Scenic Drive.

220. A picture taken at the time of the closing of Cwmcarn Colliery in 1968. Pictured from left to right are Glyn Thomas, Jimmy Winkle, Billy Pearce, Jim Barton, Ivor Jones, ?, Reg Jones (locally known as 'Spoons) with the goat, ?.

221. The location is Factory Trip Cottages, Cwmcarn in 1953 and the houses are decorated to celebrate the Queen's Coronation. First prize for the best dressed house was won by the Griffiths family.

222. The picture from the 1940s shows the Castle Inn Darts Team, Pontywaun. Back, from left to right: Tommy Greenslade, Mel Morgan, Les Strange, Edgar Strange, Harold Griffiths (Canon), Reg Beckington, Charlie Parker, Jack Crabb, Mick Donaghue, ?, Con Simmonds, Richard Williams, Tom Greenslade and Ivor Brimble. Seated: Reg Richards, Mr. Fred Stevens (Landlord), Roy Ashman and Lou Barnes.

223. Newport Road Cwmcarn, and two of the premises at the bottom of the road are Jack Hatfields Bike Shop and the Park Hall Cinema. In the front at the right can be seen J.W. Ward Newsagent and Tobacconist.

224. Staites Billiard Hall, Cwmcarn owned by William and Margaret Staite of Factory Trip, Cwmcarn during the 1920s and early 1930s. It was closed down in the 1960s and later demolished; the picture shows Mrs. Staite stood outside the building. Mr. and Mrs. Staite's nephew was Royden Jandrell who they brought up from a boy. Royden later became a Welsh Champion Billiard player and British Legion Champion.

Acknowledgements

I would like to extend my appreciation to each and every person within the community who contributed to this publication in numerous ways. My work would have been impossible to achieve without the help from the people in our valley. If I have left anyone out I sincerely apologise.

Robert Adams, Mr. Allen, Chris Barber, Mary Booton, Mr. Keith Beddis, Mrs. M. Bert, Ian Bray, Mr. & Mrs. Brooks, Mrs. Mary Butler, Mrs. Jill Carpenter, Margaret & Graham Cook, John Cornwell, Margaret Churcher, Mr. Clive Daniels, Andrew & Carole Davies, Lee Davies, Dorothy Davies, Mary & Danny Davies, Trudy & Haydn Davies, Marjorie Davies, Mrs. Davies, Mr. Deverell, Mrs. Dorman, Mr. Dennis Edwards, Marie & John English, Mrs. Ivy Evans (nee Parker), Irene & Gwyn Francis, Nora & Ted Grainger, Mrs. Graves (Newbridge Comprehensive), Dr. Madeline Grey, Violet Griffiths, Veronica, Glyn & Gail Howells, Bill Hammet, Dawn & Gary Hewlett, Linda Halfpenny, Mrs. Halfpenny, Mr. Bill Hammet, Val & Dennis Hodges, Jim Hawkesford, Mavis & Horace Hopkins, Sian & Phillip Hipkiss, Mrs. Hall, Elizabeth Jane Hall, Arthur Harris, Catherine & Brian Harris, Fred Hicks, Roger Haines, Billy Harris, Danny (Ice Cream Man), Sandra James, Mrs. Pat James, Mrs. Jandrell, Leighton Jenkins, Reg Jones (Spoons), Teresa Jennings, Knight Bros., Mr. Leonard, Mrs. Lovell (Treowen), Mrs. Lovell (Hafodyrynys), Mrs. Ada Lovell, Dennis Lewis, Sally & Colin Lloyd, Anne Mainwaring, Michael Matthews, Mrs. Myfanny Morrisey, Newbridge Comprehensive School, Mrs. Molly Partridge, Pantside Primary School, Pentwynmawr School, Mr. & Mrs. Pike, Janice & Ted Price, Andrea, Nicola & Colin Price, Terry Powell, Winifred Prior, Steve Perry, Ira Penduck, Edith & Doug Richards, Mrs. Nellie Richards, Mr. Bill Rogers, Colin Spencer, Peter Smith, Joe Selby, Mr. Graham Shipp, Mrs. Shipp, Rose Smart, Mrs. Shepherd, Mrs, Glenys Selway (nee Brookes), Mr. & Mrs. Turner, David Taylor, Gwynneth Taylor (nee Hall), Jim Taylor, Suzan Taylor, Malcolm Thomas, Mr. Tilley, Colwyn Tovey, Colin Vickers, Christine Vaughan, Mr. Vicary, the late Walter Vicary & family, Mrs, Watkins, Lynne Watkins, Horace Williams, Lee Walker & family, Harold Walkley, Phillip Walker, Mr. & Mrs. Bryn Williams, Sharon Williams, Jean & David Webb, Marion Ziomek.